# BIRD-ACIOUS

BY MELISSA STEWART

downtown bookworks

**downtown bookworks**

Ornithology Consultant: Douglas A. Lancaster

Designed by Georgia Rucker
Typeset in Bryant Pro and Warugaki

PHOTO CREDITS Front Cover: l i g h t p o e t/Shutterstock.com.
1: Sari ONeal/Shutterstock.com. 3: ©iStockPhoto/BIOphotos.
4: DM7/Shutterstock.com (*Tyrannosaurus*); Betty-Jane Leeuw/Shutterstock.com (chickadee); Christian Wilkinson/Shutterstock.com (Adélie penguins); Gualberto Becerra/Shutterstock.com (toucan).
5: Stocktrek Images/SuperStock (Archaeopteryx rendering); Vladimir Sazonov/Shutterstock.com (Archaeopteryx fossil); Stephen Coburn/Shutterstock.com (ducks); Sekar B/Shutterstock.com (roadrunner).
6: ©DeAgostini/SuperStock (all). 7: Sam DCruz/Shutterstock.com. 8: Meister Photos/Shutterstock.com (cassowary); Jay Bo/Shutterstock.com (Kori bustard). 9: Armin Rose/Shutterstock.com (wandering albatross); S. Cooper Digital/Shutterstock.com (emu); Gentoo Multimedia Limited/Shutterstock.com (emperor penguins).
10: Birdiegal/Shutterstock.com. 11: ©FLPA/SuperStock (bee hummingbird flight, sitting); StevenRussellSmithPhotos/Shutterstock.com (ruby-throated hummingbird). 12–13: Repina Valeriya/Shutterstock.com (background). 12: kzww/Shutterstock.com (contour feather); CDC/Janice Carr (up close feather); Andrzej Tokarski/Shutterstock.com (tail feather). 13: schankz/Shutterstock.com (down feather); Pakhnyushcha/Shutterstock.com (chick); KennStilger47/Shutterstock.com (turkey); Critterbiz/Shutterstock.com (bald eagle). 14: InkaOne/Shutterstock.com (heron); Neale Cousland/Shutterstock.com (rainbow lorikeet). 15: ©Paul Lemke/Dreamstime.com (cardinal); Alexonline/Shutterstock.com (bones). 16: loflo69/Shutterstock.com. 17: visceralimage/Shutterstock.com (bald eagle); Geanina Bechea/Shutterstock.com (mallard duck). 18: Tom Tarrant (spine-tailed swift); ©Hakoar/Dreamstime.com (arctic tern). 19: Jeff Banke/Shutterstock.com (peregrine falcon sitting); ©Minden Pictures/SuperStock (peregrine falcon flying); MLArduengo/Shutterstock.com (bar-tailed goodwit flying); Gertjan Hooijer/Shutterstock.com (bar-tailed goodwit perched). 20: phdwhite/Shutterstock.com (honey buzzard); ©stevebyland/Dreamstime.com (American woodcock). 21: Eric Isselee/Shutterstock.com (nightjar); ©Jansah/Dreamstime.com (horned grebe). 22: tezzstock/BigStockPhoto.com (Indian peacock); Mike Truchon/Shutterstock.com (northern cardinals). 23: Sari ONeal/Shutterstock.com (American goldfinch in winter); D and D Photo Sudbury/Shutterstock.com (American goldfinch in summer); ©Christian Hütter/imag/imagebroker.net/SuperStock (female Andean cock-of-the-rock); ©Hotshotsworldwide/Dreamstime.com (male Andean cock-of-the-rock). 24: Tom Reichner/Shutterstock.com (sage grouse); ©Biosphoto/SuperStock (crowned crane). 25: Pictureguy/Shutterstock.com (western grebes); Mariko Yuki/Shutterstock.com

(blue-footed booby). 26: Daniel Zuckerkandel/Shutterstock.com (common mures nest); David Thyberg/Shutterstock.com (common mures); H. C. Kyllingstad/Science Source (eggs). 27: ©Bob Suir/Dreamstime.com (sociable weavers nest); Karel Gallas/Shutterstock.com (sociable weavers); Petrova Maria/Shutterstock.com (sociable weavers nest close-up); ©Biosphoto/SuperStock (emperor penguins, mallee fowl close-up); Mitch Reardon/Science Source (mallee fowl). 28: ©iStockPhoto.com/Lauradyoung (bluebirds); Kimberley McClard/Shutterstock.com (killdeer). 29: ©iStockPhoto.com/GP232 (geese); Karel Gallas/Shutterstock.com (swans). 30: Steve Byland/Shutterstock.com (sparrow); Rosalie Kreulen/Shutterstock.com (hummingbird). 31: ©Wayne Lynch/All Canada Photos/SuperStock (giant petrel); mountainpix/Shutterstock.com (toucan).
32: Corinna Rodriguez/Shutterstock.com (great blue heron); apiguide/Shutterstock.com (rhinoceros hornbill); ©Minden Pictures/SuperStock (red crossbill). 33: coronado/Shutterstock.com (pelican); Glenn Price/Shutterstock.com (curlew); visceralimage/Shutterstock.com (eagle). 34: john austin/Shutterstock.com (rainbow lorikeet); ©Joan Egert/Dreamstime.com (green woodpecker); ©FLPA/SuperStock (green woodpecker's tongue); Nicola Gavin/Photos.com (African gray parrot). 35: ©Wayne Lynch/All Canada Photos/SuperStock. 36: neelsky/Shutterstock.com (jacana); ©Bruce Macqueen/Dreamstime.com (chickadee). 37: ©Keesd/Dreamstime.com (pheasant); ©age fotostock/SuperStock (duck feet below water); pudding/BigStockPhoto.com (duck feet above water). 38: raulbaenacasado/Shutterstock.com. 39: Cather of Light, Inc./Shutterstock.com; TIM LAMAN/National Geographic Creative. 40: Dima Fadeev (palm cockatoo); Minden Pictures/SuperStock (woodpecker finch). 41: Natursports/Shutterstock.com (heron); Rob Kemp/Shutterstock.com (carrion crow). 42: Iv Nikolny/Shutterstock.com (African secretary bird close-up); Federico Veronesi/Gallo Images/Getty Images (African secretary bird); Barry B. Doyle/Flickr/Getty Images (harpy eagle). 43: bikeriderlondon/Shutterstock.com (owl eating); ©Juniors/SuperStock (owl wings spread).
44: Angel DiBilio/Shutterstock.com (owl); Norman Bateman/Shutterstock.com (owl); picturepartners/Shutterstock.com (owl pellet). 46: ©iStockPhoto.com/BatGirl11. 47: ©NHPA/SuperStock (bones); sonsam/Shutterstock.com (vole); Katrina Leigh/Shutterstock.com (mouse); Eric Isselee/Shutterstock.com (mole); Stanislau, CSU, U.S. Fish and Wildlife Service (shrew).
48: ©2013 Natalya Zahn/www.natalya.com. Back cover: Marina Jay/Shutterstock.com (owl); D and D Photo Sudbury/Shutterstock.com (American goldfinch in summer); Repina Valeriya/Shutterstock.com (background).

Printed in China, July 2013

ISBN 978-1-935703-90-7

10 9 8 7 6 5 4 3 2 1

Downtown Bookworks Inc.
285 West Broadway
New York, NY 10013

www.dtbwpub.com

# CONTENTS

# BIRDASAURUS

What does a tyrannosaur have in common with a chickadee? More than you might think.

Most scientists believe that birds are the modern relatives of small meat-eating dinosaurs. Those hungry little hunters belonged to a group of dinosaurs called theropods. *Tyrannosaurus rex* was a theropod, too!

One of Earth's earliest birds was called the archaeopteryx, which means "ancient wing." The crow-sized creature lived around 150 million years ago. It had feathers and could fly, but not as well as modern birds.

Archaeopteryx fossils have been found in what is now Germany.

Adélie penguins live in freezing-cold Antarctica.

Colorful toucans live in hot, humid, tropical rain forests.

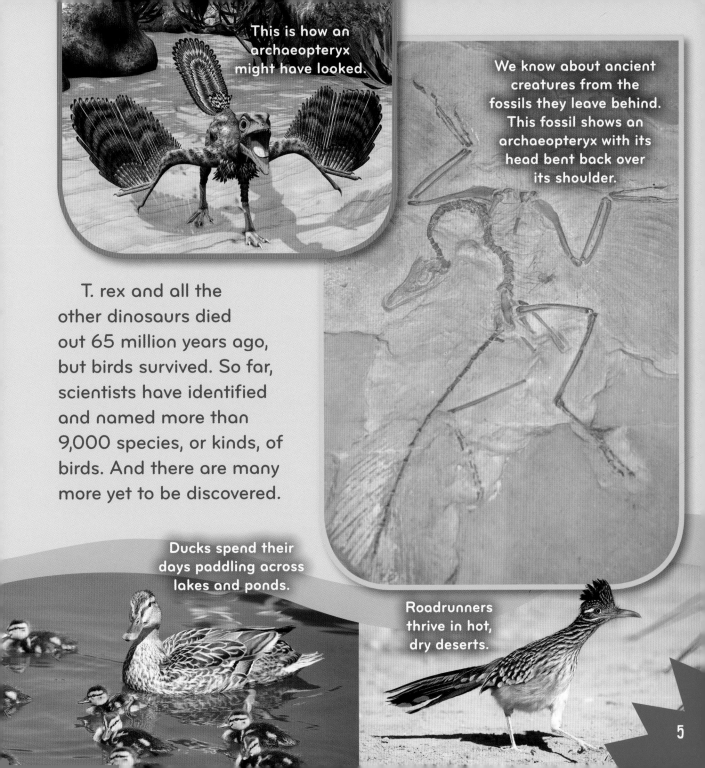

This is how an archaeopteryx might have looked.

We know about ancient creatures from the fossils they leave behind. This fossil shows an archaeopteryx with its head bent back over its shoulder.

T. rex and all the other dinosaurs died out 65 million years ago, but birds survived. So far, scientists have identified and named more than 9,000 species, or kinds, of birds. And there are many more yet to be discovered.

Ducks spend their days paddling across lakes and ponds.

Roadrunners thrive in hot, dry deserts.

# THE BIGGEST BIRDS

The biggest bird alive today is the ostrich. It can grow up to 8 feet (2 m) tall and weigh as much as 300 pounds (136 kg). The big bird may not be able to lift its body into the air, but it doesn't have any trouble getting around. Ostriches can run up to 43 miles (69 km) an hour.

The elephant bird was the largest bird ever to live on Earth. Like the ostrich, it had small wings and couldn't fly. The giant creature could be more than 10 feet (3 m) tall and weigh up to 600 pounds (272 kg). It lived on Madagascar, an island off the southeast coast of Africa.

*Argentavis,* the largest flying bird of all time, lived about 5 million years ago. It weighed about 160 pounds (73 kg), and its wings stretched more than 24 feet (7 m). Wow!

ELEPHANT BIRD

OSTRICH

HUMAN

CHICKEN

Elephant birds became extinct about 400 years ago.

Ostriches live in small herds on African grasslands and in deserts. They usually eat plants, but sometimes snack on insects and lizards.

8 FEET TALL!

# MORE BIG BIRDS

Some large birds, like the cassowary, stay on the ground. Others, like the kori bustard and the wandering albatross, are able to fly.

The 125-pound (57 kg) **cassowary** lives in the rain forests of Australia. The shy, flightless fruit eater is usually a peaceful bird. But if it feels threatened — look out! It can launch a violent attack with its sharp nails and deadly kick.

The **kori bustard** spends most of its time on the ground, picking grasshoppers, beetles, and caterpillars out of tall African grasses. Sometimes, it chases down lizards and snakes.

The 25-pound (11 kg) wandering albatross is one of the world's best fliers. With a 12-foot (4 m) wingspan, it can glide through the air for hours without flapping its wings. These big birds spend most of their lives in the air.

The emu is about the same size as a cassowary, and it also lives in Australia. But it has a lot more in common with the ostrich. Emus eat plants and insects, and they can race across their grassland home. What can emus do that ostriches can't? Swim.

Emperor penguins live in chilly Antarctica, and both parents go for weeks without food so that their chick has a better chance at survival. An emperor penguin may weigh as much as 88 pounds (40 kg).

9

# THE SMALLEST BIRDS

More than 300 kinds of hummingbirds live in wooded areas in North and South America. How do these small, colorful birds get where they want to go? They whiz through the air at more than 30 miles (48 km) per hour. Hummingbirds zip forward and then stutter as they turn. They can also fly backward and hover in one spot.

The Anna's hummingbird lives along the Pacific coast of the United States and southern Canada. It's the only North American hummer that doesn't fly south in the winter.

To reach their favorite food—sugary nectar—hummingbirds dip their long, slender bills deep inside flowers. Then they lap up the sweet juice with their tiny tongues.

Bee hummingbird

ACTUAL SIZE!

The bee hummingbird is the smallest bird in the world. It's smaller than most butterflies and weighs less than a nickel. Females lay pea-size eggs in tiny, cup-shaped nests made of bark, lichen, and spiderwebs.

The ruby-throated hummingbird spends its summers in the eastern part of North America. Besides nectar, it feeds on insects. It catches flies and mosquitoes in midair and picks small prey out of spiderwebs.

# FEATHERS UP CLOSE

## CONTOUR FEATHER

The vane on either side of the shaft is made of hundreds of small, hairlike barbs.

Magnified view of a feather

Contour feathers have a stiff, hollow shaft in the center.

Branching out from each barb are tiny hooks called barbules. The barbules hold each barb together so air can't flow between them.

Feathers make birds special. No other animals have them.

Most birds have thousands of feathers covering their bodies, but those feathers aren't all the same. Some feathers help birds stay dry and warm. Others help them hide from predators or attract mates.

**Contour feathers** cover most of a bird's body. They give a bird its shape and color. The long contour feathers on a bird's wings are called flight feathers. They lift a bird up and move it forward. **Tail feathers** help a bird steer, slow down, and keep its balance.

Tail feather

Down feather

Below the contour feathers, soft, fluffy **down feathers** keep a bird warm by trapping body heat next to its skin.

When a chick hatches, its body is covered with down feathers. Contour feathers grow in over time.

An adult wild turkey has about 3,500 feathers. It uses its flight feathers to fly up to 55 miles (89 km) per hour.

Bald eagle

A bird spends a lot of time preening, or taking care of its feathers. It uses its feet and beak to comb the feathers so they lie flat. When positioned correctly, the feathers act like a waterproof coat. Preening also removes dirt and insects from feathers.

13

# BUILT FOR FLIGHT

To take off and stay in the air, birds need a lightweight body. Luckily, birds have some special features that allow them to weigh less than other animals of the same size.

Most animals have teeth and jaws for eating, but not birds. A bird's beak is sharp enough to grab insects and tough enough to crack seeds, but it weighs very little.

A female mammal carries developing young inside her body. If a female bird had to do that, she'd be too heavy to fly. Thank goodness for eggs!

Tricolored heron

Rainbow lorikeets

Does a bird have ears? You bet! But the openings are hidden under the feathers on its head. This streamlined body design helps a bird cruise through the sky.

A bird has lungs just like you, but it also has nine air sacs. The sacs move extra air through a bird's lungs, so it gets all the oxygen it needs to fly. The air sacs also help make the bird's body lightweight.

The shape of a bird's wings can tell you how it flies. A cardinal's short wings are perfect for taking off quickly and flying in short bursts.

A bird's bones are thin and some have pockets of empty space inside.

# UP, UP, AND AWAY!

Like an airplane, a bird must take off before
it can fly. Most birds jump off a perch. A bird
spreads its wings and flaps them up and down.
The curved shape of the wings lifts the bird up
into the sky. To land, a bird stops flapping its
wings and spreads them wide. Then it uses its tail
to slow down and steer to a safe landing spot.

White stork

TAKING OFF

# SOARING

Bald eagle

Most birds flap their wings as they fly, but an eagle can soar, or glide, through the air.

# LANDING

Mallard duck

# SUPER FLIERS

Of the more than 9,000 types of birds that scientists have discovered, all but 40 can fly. Some, like the black francolin, fly only in short bursts when they are threatened. But others are masters of the sky.

Cheetahs can reach a top speed of 64 miles (103 km) per hour. Sailfish can swim across the open ocean at 68 miles (109 km) per hour. But the spine-tailed swift puts them both to shame. Long wings and a barrel-shaped body help it cruise through the air at up to 217 miles (349 km) per hour.

Spine-tailed swift

Each year, the **Arctic tern** travels more than 44,300 miles (71,294 km) from its summer home in the Arctic to its winter home in Antarctica and back. That's the world's longest migration.

In its 30-year life, the Arctic tern flies more than 1.5 million miles (2.4 million km). That's the distance to the moon and back—three times.

Arctic tern

When the **peregrine falcon** spots a potential meal, it hurls its body through the air at more than 200 miles (322 km) per hour. It cannot fly that fast all the time, but it sure can dive!

Peregrine falcon

During its migration, the Arctic tern stops regularly to rest and refuel. But the **bar-tailed godwit** doesn't take a break. It wins first prize for the longest nonstop flight by traveling the 7,000 miles (11,265 km) between New Zealand and Alaska in eight days straight.

Bar-tailed godwit

19

# FEATHER FUNCTIONS

Birds couldn't fly without their feathers, but that's not all feathers can do. Look at the fascinating ways these birds use their feathers.

When an **American woodcock** wants to attract a mate, it uses its feathers both to fly and to make noise. Just after sunset, a male American woodcock spirals upward and makes a twittering whistle with his feathers. When the bird is about 250 feet (76 m) high, it hovers briefly and then plummets downward in a zigzagging dive.

A **honey buzzard's** favorite foods are bees and wasps. Tightly overlapping feathers protect the bird's face from painful stings.

The horned grebe is only colorful during mating season. In the winter, its feathers are black and white.

A **horned grebe** usually eats fish, frogs, and insects, but sometimes it snacks on something surprising— its own feathers. Adults feed feathers to their chicks, too. As the feathers break down, they form a feltlike material that protects the bird's stomach from sharp fish bones.

A **nightjar** hunts in the dark. Small, stiff feathers around its mouth act like whiskers. These bristlelike feathers help the nightjar detect the movements of insects and other prey, so the bird knows when to snap its bill shut.

# FAB OR DRAB

Many male birds like to show off for the less-colorful females. In the bird world, bright colors and big, fancy feathers send a message to females, saying: "I'm strong and healthy, so I'll make a great dad."

How does an Indian peacock impress the ladies? By fanning out his huge, colorful tail feathers and letting the round eyespots shimmer in the sun.

Female **northern cardinals** (left) are light brown, so they blend in with their forest surroundings. The bright, bold males (right) really stand out. And that's the point. As far as the females are concerned, redder is better.

A male American goldfinch's colors change with the seasons. In winter (left), he has a tan head and a white belly. But in early spring (right), he loses his feathers and grows bright yellow ones for the summer mating season.

A female Andean cock-of-the-rock has a dull orange-brown body (left). But she looks for a mate with a brilliant orange body (right).

23

# LET'S DANCE!

At mating time, male birds have just one goal—to get a female's attention. Some males do this by strutting their stuff.

How does a male sage grouse attract a mate? He puffs up his feathers and sashays around her like a runway model. All the while, he makes a loud popping noise by blowing up air sacs on his chest.

A male crowned crane is a tall, proud bird. And he really knows how to put on a show. When he spots a female, he waves his wings, bobs his head, and hops up and down as he circles around her. What a sight!

24

After a **western grebe** picks a mate, the couple dances together. They shake their heads back and forth and call out with harsh, machine-gun-like sounds. Then they rush forward in unison, necks curved, bodies upright. It looks like the birds are running on top of the water.

A **blue-footed booby** spreads his wings wide and whistles. Then he stomps, shuffles, and slides his bright-blue feet. If the female likes what she sees, she joins the dance. It's her way of saying, "We belong together."

25

# GETTING READY FOR BABY

Common murres

Common murre eggs

After birds mate, they look for the perfect spot to raise their family. Most birds build nests in trees or shrubs. Because these nests are safe from enemies, the eggs are often one solid color.

Other birds build their nests on the ground. They usually lay gray or light-brown eggs with darker spots, speckles, streaks, and squiggles. The markings help the eggs blend in with their surroundings. A few kinds of birds lay their eggs directly on the ground or on rocky ledges. Common murres lay eggs on cliffs high above the sea. Each egg has a pointy end, so if an adult bird accidently bumps into it, the egg rolls in a circle instead of tumbling over the edge.

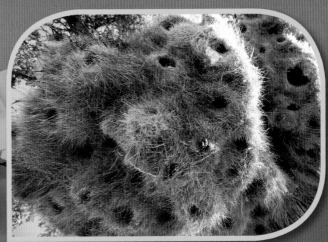

Groups of **sociable weavers** work together to build and maintain huge nests that can house more than 200 birds. The nests are like apartment buildings—each pair of birds gets its own separate chamber.

A mama **mallee fowl** buries her eggs in a giant compost heap. As the plants rot, the pile gives off heat that keeps the eggs warm. Each day, the male sticks his bill deep into the heap to make sure it's just the right temperature.

A female **emperor penguin** lays one egg at a time. Her mate balances the egg on his feet and drapes his belly over it, so it won't freeze. What a devoted dad!

27

# BRINGING UP BABY

Chicks that develop inside eggs laid in safe treetop nests are usually helpless when they hatch. Their eyes are closed and they have no feathers at all. Their parents must feed them for several weeks until they learn to fly.

To keep their home neat and clean, **bluebird** parents pick up their chicks' poop and dump it far from the nest.

When a predator gets too close to a **killdeer's** nest, the brave mama bird pretends she has a broken wing. She drags herself across the ground, leading the enemy away from her helpless chicks. Just as the attacker is about to lunge, the killdeer shoots into the air and flies out of harm's way.

Young ducks and geese, like these Canada geese, follow the first moving object they see— usually their mom.

Chicks that hatch in nests on the ground spend more time inside their eggs. When they burst into the world, they can see and hear. A layer of fluffy feathers keeps them warm. These chicks usually start hunting for themselves within a day of hatching.

Mother swans carry their young on their back until the chicks are able to swim on their own.

# EATING LIKE A BIRD

You probably eat about 2 pounds (1 kg) of food each day. Food gives you all the energy you need to live and grow. Birds get energy from food, too. They need it to build nests, lay eggs, and keep their bodies warm. But flying takes the most energy of all.

If you ate like a chickadee, you'd chow down about 70 hamburgers every single day! Now you know why you see birds visiting backyard bird feeders all day long.

Birds and people need more than just food to make energy. We both need oxygen—one of the gases in air. Because a **sparrow's** body needs so much energy, it breathes about four times faster than we do.

Why does a **hummingbird's** heart beat about nine times faster than yours? So it can pump lots more blood to its cells. Blood contains the food and oxygen that cells need to make energy.

After gorging on a dead seal or whale, a giant petrel is too heavy to fly. Most of the time, it naps on the beach while its body digests the meal. But if an enemy attacks, the clever bird has a backup plan. It vomits until its body is light enough to take flight.

Unlike the giant petrel, the **toucan** eats mostly fruit. The sawlike edges of a toucan's enormous beak can tear large fruits into pieces that are small enough to swallow.

Giant petrel

# BEAKS TELL TALES

Beaks come in a variety of sizes and shapes. They can be big or small, straight or hooked. You can tell what a bird eats by looking at its beak.

A **great blue heron** uses its long, sharp bill to stab fish and frogs.

The brightly colored structure on top of a **rhinoceros hornbill's** beak is perfectly designed to knock ripe fruit off rain-forest trees.

A **red crossbill** uses its beak to pull tasty seeds out of cones and fruits.

An **eagle** uses its hooked beak like a knife. After the hunter catches a fish, it uses its beak to strip away a fish's scaly skin and pick meat off the bones.

A pelican uses its beak to scoop fish out of the ocean. After the water drains out, the bird swallows its dinner.

A **curlew** uses its long, thin beak to probe sandy soil for worms, insects, and shrimp.

# TERRIFIC TONGUES

Birds may not have teeth, but they do have tongues. And their tongues serve all kinds of purposes—from collecting food to making sounds.

Sharp spikes and sticky spit on the tip of a green woodpecker's long tongue help it nab insects inside a hole in a tree. When the bird is done eating, it slides its tongue into a groove that wraps around the outside of its skull beneath the skin.

A rainbow lorikeet has tiny hairlike brushes on the tip of its tongue. When the little bird is hungry, it sticks its tongue deep into a flower and soaks up sweet nectar and powdery pollen.

Close-up of a green woodpecker's long tongue

An African gray parrot's thick, swollen tongue looks a lot like yours. It helps the bird control the movement of air, allowing it to make noises that sound like human words.

A penguin's tongue is covered with sharp spikes that point backward, toward its throat. The spikes stop slippery, slimy fish from sliding out of the bird's mouth.

35

# FANCY FEET

When a **jacana** spreads out its long toes, it can walk across water lilies in search of insects, snails, and seeds.

A bird's beak and feet are on opposite ends of its body, but they have something in common. Just like a bird's beak, its feet can help you figure out what it eats and how it hunts. For example, a chickadee often holds a seed between its toes and pecks at it or bangs it against a hard surface until the shell breaks open.

Chickadee

A **pheasant** uses its tough toes to scratch the ground, stirring up insects and other tasty treats.

A **duck's** webbed feet are perfect for paddling through the water as the bird hunts for insects and small fish. Every now and then, the bird dives underwater to nibble on plants.

# TRICKS OF THE TRADE

Because birds are small animals whose meat is tasty, they have many enemies. Most of the time, they can wing their way to safety. But sometimes, they need a little bit of extra protection.

Mama **hoopoes** know just how to convince predators to look elsewhere for food. They produce a nasty-smelling oil that they rub all over their bodies and on their chicks. The stench of rotting meat makes most hungry predators lose their appetite.

The **hooded pitohui** spends its days gobbling up beetles that are full of poison. And it doesn't bother the bird a bit. Over time, the poison builds up in its feathers and skin, making it poisonous, too.

When a hungry fox or coyote stumbles upon burrowing owl chicks in their underground nest, the chicks make a loud hissing noise that sounds just like a rattlesnake. They can't fly yet, but their hissing is enough to send most predators scampering out of sight.

HISSSSSS

HISSSSSSS

HISSSSSSS

# BRAINY BIRDS

Scientists used to think people were the only animals smart enough to use tools, but now they know better. It turns out that elephants, chimps, dolphins, and dingoes all have the know-how to put tools to work. So do some birds.

A **woodpecker finch** uses sharp cactus spines to pry grubs out of crevices in tree bark.

At mating time, a male **palm cockatoo** uses a twig to drum on a hollow tree. Scientists aren't sure if the sound attracts females or lets other males know they should stay away.

The carrion crow will perch near a traffic light and wait for it to turn red. Then it will hop onto the road and place a hard nut in front of a car tire. The car drives over the nut and cracks the shell open. When the road is clear, the crow hops out and gobbles up the nut.

A heron might use insects, berries, or twigs to catch its dinner. It tosses the bait into the water and waits. When a curious fish comes to check out the bait, the heron attacks.

# HUNTERS BY DAY...

From dawn to dusk, 300 species of raptors rule the sky. Their huge eyes, hooked beaks, and sharp claws make them skilled predators. The hungry hunters soar through the air, searching for prey on the ground. When they spot a target, they swoop down and grab the unsuspecting victim with their feet.

The **African secretary bird** stalks its prey on the ground. When the powerful bird spots a snake, it attacks, pecking with its beak and stomping with its feet until the snake is dead.

The huge **harpy eagle** lives in the rain forests of Central and South America. It feeds on sloths, monkeys, and other medium-size mammals.

# AND NIGHT

As the sun goes down, hawks, eagles, falcons, and vultures drift off to sleep, but owls are just waking up. These nighttime birds of prey use sight and sound to locate food. Then they go in for the kill.

A barn owl can eat up to 1,000 mice a year.

There are more than 150 species of owls alive today. The most common species is the barn owl.

# WHAT A WASTE!

You make several trips to the bathroom every day. Sometimes you poop. Sometimes you pee. But a bird's body makes just one kind of waste—a thick, white liquid with small, dark bits of dung. Like our pee and poop, a bird's droppings are full of things they eat but their bodies don't need.

**Turkey vultures** live in sizzling-hot, dry areas. Believe it or not, these big birds cool themselves off by spraying droppings on their legs. Yuck!

If you compare an owl's droppings to those of other birds, you'll notice something strange. Owl droppings don't contain very many dark bits of dung. That's because owls regurgitate, or throw up, most of the materials they can't digest.

An average owl upchucks two thumb-size pellets every day.

# YOUR VERY OWN OWL PELLET

The owl pellet that comes with this book is from a barn owl. Your pellet has been heat-treated—baked at 250°F (121°C) for four hours— in order to kill bacteria. Prior to landing in your book, the pellet was stored in mothballs, which you may still be able to smell.

### HOW TO DISSECT AN OWL PELLET

• Soak the owl pellet in warm water for about five minutes.

• Place the softened pellet on a clean paper towel.

• Use tweezers or two toothpicks or chopsticks to slowly and gently pull the mass of materials apart. Be very careful using your hands, as some of the tiny bones you find might be pointy.

• As soon as you spot a bone, put your tools down for a minute and look closely at what's nearby. That's the best way to identify the bone. The illustrations on page 48 can also help you figure out what you're looking at.

• Wash your hands with warm, soapy water after handling the pellet.

An owl's favorite foods include mice, shrews, voles, moles, and other small mammals. Sometimes they eat small birds. That's why they spit up pellets filled with fur, feathers, and tiny bones. Sometimes, they contain seeds or the hard outer skins of insects. Many owl pellets contain one animal, but some may have two or even three.

VOLE

You'll find bones and teeth like these inside an owl pellet.

The largest bone in the pellet will be a skull.

Near a skull, you might find a jaw. It might still have teeth attached. The long front teeth at the front of the mouth are called incisors.

Incisors are often yellow in color. Rodents use their incisors to gnaw on wood, bite into things, and defend themselves.

A rodent's back teeth are used for grinding food.

If you see a row of similar bones, they might be ribs.

MOLE

MOUSE

SHREW

# IDENTIFY THE BONES

As you sift through your owl pellet, you will uncover lots of little bones. Start by identifying any skulls you find. The bones near the skull are most likely from the same animal. Here are the most common types of skulls to find in an owl pellet.

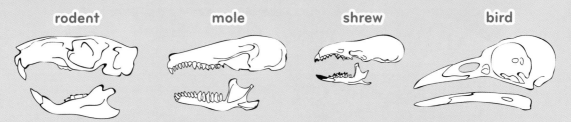

rodent          mole          shrew          bird

Owls eat many kinds of rodents, including mice, rats, and voles. The illustrations below will help you identify the small bones you find in your owl pellet.

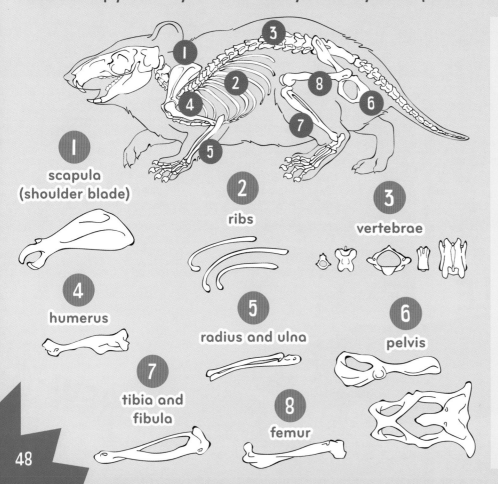

1 scapula (shoulder blade)

2 ribs

3 vertebrae

4 humerus

5 radius and ulna

6 pelvis

7 tibia and fibula

8 femur

**BONE UP ON BIRDS!**
To learn more, check out these resources.

**BOOKS**
Judge, Lita. *Bird Talk: What Birds Are Saying and Why.* New York: Flashpoint/Roaring Brook, 2012.

Laubach, Christyna M., René Laubach, and Charles W.G. Smith. p *Raptor! A Kid's Guide to Birds of Prey.* North Adams, MA: Storey Books, 2002.

Stewart, Melissa. *Feathers: Not Just for Flying.* Watertown, MA: Charlesbridge, 2014.

Weidensaul, Scott. *National Audubon Society First Field Guide: Birds.* New York: Scholastic, 1998.

**WEBSITES**
**All About Birds**
allaboutbirds.org

**National Geographic**
animals.nationalgeographic.com/animals/birds